GA

MW00749200

Fast
Pasta

Anne O'Donovan
in association with
Penguin Books

A PENGUIN POCKET SERIES BOOK

First published in 1994 by
Anne O'Donovan Pty Ltd
Level 3, 171 La Trobe Street Melbourne 3000

Reprinted 1994 (twice)
Reprinted 1995 (twice)
Reprinted 1996
Copyright text © Gabriel Gaté, 1992

Written with Angie Burns Gaté
Designed and illustrated by Lynn Twelftree
Typeset by Abb-typesetting Pty Ltd, Collingwood, Victoria
Printed by McPherson's Printing Group
Distributed by Penguin Books Australia Ltd

National Library of Australia
Cataloguing-in-publication entry

Gaté, Gabriel, 1955
    Gabriel Gaté's, fast pasta.

    Includes index.
    ISBN 0 14 024303 8.

    1. Cookery (Pasta). I. Title. II. Title: fast pasta. (Series:
Penguin pocket series).

641.822

CONTENTS

Introduction   4
Choosing and cooking pasta   5
How much pasta to cook   5
Pasta – all shapes and sizes   6

Favourite sauces   10
Great classics   18
Really fast pasta   26
Pasta for every day   40
Pasta for special occasions   78
Asian noodles   96
Couscous   120

Index   128

INTRODUCTION

Many Italian, Asian and North African people eat pasta, noodles or couscous every day. These staple foods are made from flour and water, and sometimes, especially with fresh pasta and noodles, eggs are added. We prepare them in many different ways and never seem to tire of them.

For this pocket book I have selected fast pasta dishes, some of which you may be familiar with, as well as others that are less common and more exotic, for more special occasions. I have included some information about the different types of pasta shapes available but I suggest you experiment. I have also included recipes for Asian noodle dishes and for these it is best to shop at Asian grocery stores, or the Asian section of your supermarket, to buy the 'real thing' if you want your dishes to have the authentic Asian flavour.

I hope you will adopt my suggestions, feeling free to alter recipes to suit your own taste. Most importantly, if you have children, share these recipes and help them understand what makes a good dish.

Best wishes and happy cooking.

Gabriel Gate

CHOOSING AND COOKING PASTA

The range of pasta and noodles now available on the supermarket shelves is quite impressive – there are virtually hundreds of varieties. In the recipes I have suggested specific pasta shapes, but you should feel free to use whatever suits you best. It is nice to use fresh pasta but there are excellent types of dried pasta that are sometimes better than fresh ones, for example, spaghetti.

Pasta should be cooked in a large volume of lightly salted, boiling water and cooking times vary from one type of pasta to another. Instructions are usually printed on the pack of dried pasta. Fresh pasta cooks more quickly – ask your shopkeeper for the suggested cooking time when you buy your pasta. Instructions for Asian noodles and couscous are usually printed on the pack.

Once the pasta is placed in the water, stir it briefly to prevent sticking. Well-cooked pasta is still a little firm and just moist in the centre. Bite through a piece and see for yourself. When well cooked, pasta is described as *al dente* – Italian for 'on the tooth', meaning firm. When cooking pasta, have a colander on hand and take the pasta pot to the sink. Add about one cup of water to the pot to stop further cooking before draining the pasta well and tossing it with a seasoning or sauce.

HOW MUCH PASTA TO COOK

As a general rule, cook about 75–125 g (3–4 oz) of dried pasta, or 125–175 g (4–6 oz) of fresh pasta per person for an average main course serving.

PASTA – All shapes and sizes

Asian egg noodles
Asian noodles are made from the same ingredients as many types of Italian pasta, i.e. flour, water and eggs. Available fresh or dried at supermarkets or Asian grocers. The dried type is sold in compressed packs.

Bucatini
A large, hollow spaghetti which is delicious with thick sauces.

Capelli d'angelo
Long and wispy, hence the name 'angel's hair'; it is mostly used in soups.

Cellophane noodles
These long transparent noodles are made from the starch paste of mung beans or other Asian pulses. The cooking is either very short or they need only to be soaked in hot water before being used.

Conchiglie
Short pasta, shaped like shell fish. They come in many different shapes. The small ones are good in soup, and the large ones are excellent with chunky sauces.

Couscous
Made from wheat, this North African staple is made with flour and water and is shaped into tiny pellets. Commercial couscous cooks quickly and instructions are on the pack.

Farfalle
In the shape of a butterfly, or bow-tie, this short pasta was my favourite as a child. Great as a quick meal mixed with leftovers.

Fettucine
Long and flat like a ribbon, fettucine is wider than spaghetti and thinner than tagliatelle. It is sometimes made with eggs and is one of the most popular of all fresh pasta.

Gnocchi
Small dumplings usually made with mashed potato and flour (and sometimes eggs), they are very popular as a light, quick meal.

Linguine
Looks like flat spaghetti and means 'tongs'.

Long fusilli
Long, springy pasta, thicker than spaghetti and delicious with chunky ingredients.

Maccheroni
We call it 'macaroni'. These short, hollow tubes come in different lengths and are a popular family pasta, which children love to eat with cheese.

Orecchiette
A small ear-shaped pasta, often served with broccoli or anchovies in the sauce.

Penne
A short, tubular pasta with ends that are cut like the nib of a pen. Delicious with sauces that become trapped in the hollow.

Ravioli
These little parcels filled with meat, cheese, seafood or vegetables, are especially lovely when freshly made.

Rice noodles
These long, dried noodles come in different shapes and are available from supermarkets and Asian grocers. They cook very quickly and some only need to be soaked in hot water before being used.

Rigatoni
A good pasta for the family. Their shape is a short, hollow tube and they are delicious with sauces. They make a suitable alternative to maccheroni.

Ruote di carro
First made in Sicily, this 'cart wheel' pasta is lovely with ingredients that get caught in the pasta.

Spaghetti
Long, thin and round, spaghetti is probably the most popular of all dried pasta.

Spaghettini
The name means 'small spaghetti'. They are delicious with flavoursome sauces and make a good substitute for noodles in Asian dishes.

Tagliatelle
Like a long, flat ribbon about 1 cm wide, they are often served with bolognese sauce in Italy.

Tortellini
A short pasta stuffed with a meat filling and folded in the shape of a navel. Popular in broths or sauces.

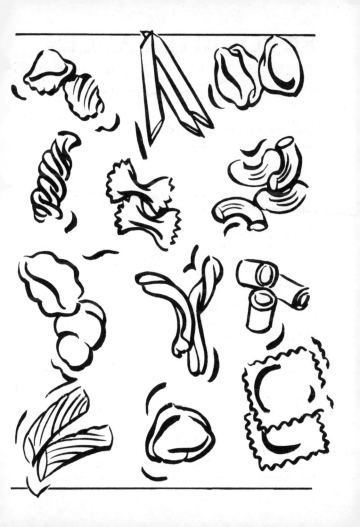

FAVOURITE SAUCES

Pesto Genovese

This is a very aromatic Italian sauce that suits most types of pasta, whether served hot or in a salad.

MAKES ABOUT 1 CUP

1 cup unblemished basil leaves
2 tbsp pine nuts
4 cloves garlic
1 tbsp grated parmesan cheese
1 tbsp grated pecorino cheese
¼ tsp salt
3 tbsp olive oil

METHOD

Wash basil, drain well and dry in a clean teatowel or kitchen paper.

Place basil, pine nuts, peeled garlic, parmesan, pecorino and salt in a food processor and blend to a paste. Add oil and blend until well combined.

If not using pesto immediately, place in a jar, cover with olive oil which will preserve it longer, seal jar and store in the refrigerator.

Mexican-bean sauce

This is a hearty, filling sauce that is ideal when the family feels like something tasty and satisfying.

SERVES 4

400 g (14 oz) can peeled tomatoes
¼ tsp cummin seeds
¼ onion, chopped
½ carrot, chopped
½ small chilli
400 g (14 oz) can beans (such as cannellini, red kidney beans)
salt and freshly ground black pepper
1 tbsp olive oil

METHOD

Place tomatoes in a saucepan with cummin seeds, onion, carrot and chilli and cook for 20 mins. Pass sauce through a mouli.

Add drained beans to tomato sauce, season with salt and pepper and stir in olive oil before serving with pasta.

Always toss the pasta very gently with the sauce.

Matriciana sauce

A spicy sauce with hot salami and chilli that can be
served with long or short pasta. You can make it a day
or two in advance and reheat it.

> ### SERVES 4
>
> **2 tbsp olive oil**
> **½ onion, chopped**
> **2 cloves garlic, chopped**
> **1½ small red chilli, finely sliced**
> **12 slices hot salami, cut into pieces**
> **about 2 cups peeled canned tomatoes**
> **freshly ground black pepper**

METHOD

Heat oil in a non-stick pan and stir-fry onion, garlic,
chilli and salami for about 3 mins.

Meanwhile, chop canned tomatoes. Add tomatoes to
pan and simmer for about 5 mins. Season with pepper
and serve.

Garlic and parsley sauce

This is a quick seasoning that we enjoy with all kinds of pasta, especially with spaghetti.

SERVES 2

1 small clove garlic, finely chopped
1 tbsp olive oil
1 tbsp chopped parsley
1 tbsp pine nuts, toasted (optional)
a small pinch of cayenne pepper
1 tsp butter
freshly ground black pepper

METHOD

In a small bowl mix garlic, olive oil, parsley, pine nuts and cayenne pepper. Gently toss this flavoured oil with your cooked pasta, adding butter, and season with pepper just before serving.

Italian tomato sauce

Make this sauce when tomatoes are sweet and aromatic. At other times of the year use bottled Italian-style tomato sauce, available in all supermarkets. You can add fresh herbs or spices of your choice to the finished sauce.

SERVES ABOUT 4

6 medium tomatoes
½ brown onion
1 stick celery
1 medium carrot
10 basil leaves
1 sprig parsley
1 clove garlic, left whole
1 tbsp olive oil
freshly ground black pepper

METHOD

Cut tomatoes, onion, celery and carrot into small pieces and place in a saucepan with basil, parsley and garlic. Cover with a lid and cook on medium heat for about 20 mins.

Remove parsley and basil and pass sauce through a mouli or fine strainer. Stir in olive oil and season with black pepper before serving.

You can keep this sauce for 2 to 3 days in the refrigerator or for at least 1 month in the freezer.

GREAT CLASSICS

Spaghetti alla carbonara

A great favourite for many. I prefer spaghetti alla carbonara not too rich, with just a little cream. Here is my version.

SERVES 4

400 g (14 oz) spaghetti
4 slices lean bacon
1 tbsp olive oil
½ tbsp red wine vinegar
2 tbsp cream
2 tbsp grated parmesan cheese
2 tbsp grated pecorino cheese
2 egg yolks
2 tbsp parsley, chopped
freshly ground black pepper

METHOD

Bring a large pot of lightly salted water to the boil and cook pasta in boiling water until *al dente*.

Meanwhile, cut bacon into small pieces and fry in olive oil for a few mins. Transfer bacon to a plate. Add vinegar to pan and bring to the boil before stirring in cream, parmesan and pecorino. Turn off heat.

Drain pasta. Place in a serving dish and toss with cream cheese sauce, egg yolks and parsley. Sprinkle bacon pieces over dish and season with black pepper just before serving.

Spaghetti with fresh seafood
(Spaghetti marinara)

You can change this dish according to what is freshest at the market or fish shop, or by using the type of seafood your family prefers. It is also good for a special occasion lunch with friends.

SERVES 2

200g (7 oz) spaghetti
1 tbsp olive oil
4 green prawns, shelled
6 scallops, washed
100 g (3½ oz) firm fish fillets, cut into
   bite-size pieces
1 tbsp brandy (optional)
1 cup Italian-style tomato sauce
salt and freshly ground black pepper
a pinch of cayenne pepper
1 clove garlic, finely chopped
1 tbsp finely cut basil or parsley

METHOD

Bring a large pot of lightly salted water to the boil and cook spaghetti in boiling water until *al dente*.

Meanwhile, heat olive oil in a non-stick pan and cook prawns, scallops and fish for about 2 mins. Transfer fish to a plate. Add brandy and tomato sauce to pan and bring to the boil. Season with salt, pepper and cayenne. Mix seafood, garlic and basil with sauce and toss gently with drained spaghetti. Serve immediately.

Spaghetti alla puttanesca

We have enjoyed this quick puttanesca sauce for many years. It is a good one to learn. Always keep a piece of parmesan cheese on hand and grate it just before serving for the freshest flavour.

SERVES 4

2 tbsp olive oil
2 cloves garlic, chopped
4 anchovy fillets, chopped
400 g (14 oz) can peeled tomatoes, chopped
12 black olives, sliced
2 tbsp chopped parsley
1 tbsp chopped fresh basil
salt and freshly ground black pepper
400 g (14 oz) spaghetti
grated parmesan cheese

METHOD

Heat oil in a non-stick pan, add garlic and anchovies and fry for 1 min. Add tomatoes and olives and bring quickly to the boil for 2 mins before stirring in parsley and basil. Season to taste with salt and pepper.

Meanwhile, cook spaghetti in a large pot of boiling salted water. Drain pasta well, toss with sauce and serve with parmesan cheese.

Macaroni au gratin

French people love this dish and often cook it when there's some leftover macaroni to be used. You can create variation in the seasoning by using different spices and herbs. It is fairly rich, so serve something light with it, such as a salad or some fruit.

SERVES 4

400 g (14 oz) cooked macaroni
salt and freshly ground black pepper
a little olive oil
2 tbsp cream
2 egg yolks
1 tsp sweet paprika
¼ tsp curry powder
4 tbsp grated Swiss-style cheese
4 tbsp dried breadcrumbs

METHOD

Season cold macaroni with salt and pepper and place in a lightly oiled gratin dish.

Preheat oven to 180°C/350°F.

In a bowl mix cream, egg yolks, paprika and curry powder. Pour this evenly over pasta. Sprinkle with grated cheese and then with breadcrumbs. Place in oven and cook for 15 mins. Place dish under a hot grill for a few mins if you wish to brown the top.

REALLY FAST PASTA

Penne with sun-dried tomatoes and basil

Sun-dried tomatoes have become very popular and the concentration of tomato flavour is very attractive. It is best, however, to use them sparingly as they can be very salty.

SERVES 2

200 g (7 oz) penne
4 sun-dried tomatoes
1 tbsp pine nuts, toasted
1 tbsp olive oil
1 tbsp finely sliced basil
freshly ground black pepper
grated parmesan cheese

METHOD

Bring a large pot of lightly salted water to the boil and cook penne until *al dente*.

Meanwhile, cut sun-dried tomatoes into long strips.

Drain cooked pasta, place in a serving dish and toss with sun-dried tomatoes, pine nuts, olive oil and basil. Season with pepper and serve with grated parmesan.

Fresh pasta takes less time to cook than dried pasta.

Macaroni with stir-fried beef

*A quick dish I cook for myself when I am on my own.
I might add a few steamed beans or broccoli and voila!
It's a meal!*

SERVES 1

100 g (3½ oz) macaroni
½ tbsp peanut oil
125 g (4½ oz) beef fillet, cut into strips
1 tsp soy sauce
a few drops of sesame oil
a little chilli paste
freshly ground black pepper
a few sprigs of coriander

METHOD

Bring a pot of lightly salted water to the boil and cook macaroni in boiling water until *al dente*.

Meanwhile, heat peanut oil in a wok and stir-fry beef for 1 min. Add soy sauce, sesame oil and a little chilli paste to taste. Toss drained pasta with meat, season with pepper and serve with sprigs of coriander on top.

Different pasta shapes have a different cooking time. Always read the cooking instructions on the pack or ask at your fresh pasta shop about cooking times.

Fast spaghetti bolognese

A traditional bolognese cooks for several hours and is delicious. This version is ideal if you are short of time as it is very quick, but it is still lovely.

SERVES 4

2 tbsp olive oil
½ onion, finely chopped
1 small carrot, finely chopped
1 stick celery, finely chopped
1 tsp dried oregano
250 g (9 oz) rump steak, freshly minced
1 cup red wine
2 cloves garlic, chopped
2 cups Italian-style tomato sauce
salt and freshly ground black pepper
400 g (14 oz) spaghetti
2 tbsp finely chopped parsley
grated parmesan cheese

METHOD

Heat oil in a non-stick pan and stir-fry onion, carrot and celery for 5 mins. Stir in oregano and minced steak and cook on high heat for 3 mins. Add wine and bring to the boil before adding garlic and tomato sauce. Leave to simmer for 15 mins. Season to taste with salt and pepper.

Meanwhile, cook spaghetti in a large volume of lightly salted, boiling water. Drain spaghetti and toss with meat sauce and parsley. Serve with parmesan cheese.

Spaghettini with ginger and chilli

Some will like this dish spicier than others. For a change, try serving it with stir-fried chicken or beef.

SERVES 4

1 tbsp peanut oil
½ onion, finely chopped
2 thin slices ginger
1 clove garlic, finely chopped
1 tsp curry powder
salt and freshly ground black pepper
400 g (14 oz) spaghettini
½ tsp chilli paste

METHOD

Heat oil in a wok or large frying pan and stir-fry
onion, ginger and garlic for a few mins. Stir in curry
powder and a little salt and pepper and cook on low
heat for 2 mins.

Meanwhile, cook spaghettini in a large pot of salted
boiling water. Drain pasta. Toss well with curry
preparation and chilli paste and serve.

Long fusilli with tuna and capers

This dish is ideal for a light lunch with a few friends or for an easy Sunday evening dinner. After such a dish I would serve a lovely mixed green salad and a good cheese.

SERVES 2

200 g (7 oz) fusilli
200 g (7 oz) can tuna in oil
1 clove garlic, chopped
2 tsp small capers
2 tbsp chopped parsley
freshly ground black pepper

METHOD

Bring a large pot of salted water to the boil and cook pasta in boiling water until *al dente*.

Drain oil from tuna and mix oil, garlic, capers and parsley with drained pasta. Season with pepper.

Sprinkle tuna over pasta just before serving.

Ricotta ravioli with ham

We often serve this dish for a weekend lunch when we feel like something hot and substantial but we are in a hurry. Note that I have included garlic and parsley, but these are optional.

SERVES 4

300–400 g (11–14 oz) ricotta ravioli
½ tbsp olive oil
1 tsp butter
3 thin slices ham, finely shredded
½ clove garlic, very finely chopped
2 tbsp chopped parsley
2 tbsp freshly grated parmesan cheese

METHOD

Bring a large saucepan of lightly salted water to the boil and cook the ravioli until soft. Drain ravioli.

In a non-stick frying pan heat olive oil and butter and stir-fry ham for 1 min before stirring in garlic and parsley. Gently toss ravioli with ham and serve with freshly grated parmesan.

Freshly grated parmesan is much more flavoursome than the pre-packaged variety.

Gnocchi with tomato and pine nuts

Our children loved gnocchi before mashed potato, and yet gnocchi are made from mashed potato and flour. It must be the texture of gnocchi they like. If you serve this dish to the very little ones, omit the pine nuts.

SERVES 4

300 g (11 oz) gnocchi
1 cup Italian-style tomato sauce
1 tsp olive oil
2 tbsp toasted pine nuts
1 tbsp grated parmesan cheese

METHOD

Bring a pot of lightly salted water to the boil and cook gnocchi until they all float on top of the water.

Meanwhile, reheat tomato sauce and olive oil.

Gently toss drained gnocchi with tomato sauce and serve sprinkled with pine nuts and parmesan.

PASTA FOR EVERY DAY

Rigatoni with soy chicken

This is a dish you can prepare best with the help of a wok. Although in this recipe I suggest using chicken fillets, you can use other cuts it you prefer a stronger flavour.

SERVES 4

300–400 g (11–14 oz) rigatoni
about 300 g chicken fillets, skinless
1 tbsp vegetable oil
1 tsp butter
1 tbsp soy sauce
a few drops of lemon juice

METHOD

Bring a large pot of lightly salted water to the boil and cook pasta in boiling water until *al dente*.

Meanwhile, cut chicken fillets into small strips.

Heat oil and butter in a wok and stir-fry chicken until just cooked. Stir in soy sauce and lemon juice, toss with drained cooked rigatoni and serve.

Tagliatelle with chicken livers

For those who love liver this is a treat. The secret of the dish is to avoid overcooking the livers or they become dry. Make sure the livers are very fresh.

SERVES 2

200 g (7 oz) tagliatelle
1 tbsp olive oil
about 150g (5½ oz) chicken livers, cleaned
¼ brown onion, finely chopped
about 30 g (1 oz) butter
salt and freshly ground black pepper
1 tbsp chopped parsley

METHOD

Bring a large pot of lightly salted water to the boil and cook pasta in boiling water until *al dente*.

Meanwhile, heat oil in a non-stick frying pan and cook livers on one side for a few mins. Add chopped onion and turn livers over. Add butter and cook livers on the other side. Season with salt and plenty of pepper.

Gently toss drained pasta with livers, onion, cooking juices and parsley and serve.

Introduce your children to the pleasures of cooking pasta.

Tagliatelle with spicy minced beef

You can make this dish quite exotic by using your favourite mix of spices. I like a touch of cummin and chilli with fresh coriander leaves.

SERVES 4

300–400 g (11–14 oz) tagliatelle
1 tbsp olive oil
½ brown onion, finely chopped
2 tsp ground cummin
300 g (11 oz) minced beef
2 tbsp Italian-style tomato sauce
salt and freshly ground black pepper
1 tsp chilli paste
a few sprigs of coriander leaves

METHOD

Bring a large pot of lightly salted water to the boil and cook pasta in boiling water until *al dente*.

Meanwhile, heat oil in a wok or frying pan and stir-fry chopped onion for 3 mins. Increase heat, add cummin and beef and stir-fry until beef has changed colour. Stir in tomato sauce and season with salt, pepper and chilli paste. Gently toss drained pasta with mince and serve with coriander leaves.

Spaghettini with fine herbs and garlic

Remember to cook the spaghettini al dente for the best result. When a dish calls for fine herbs, use fresh herbs only but don't worry if some of the herbs listed are unavailable.

SERVES 2

200 g (7 oz) spaghettini
½ tbsp olive oil
½ tbsp butter
1 tbsp finely cut basil
1 tbsp chopped parsley
1 tsp finely cut tarragon
freshly ground black pepper
a few sprigs of chervil

METHOD

Cook pasta in lightly salted, boiling water until *al dente*. Drain pasta. Place in a serving dish and toss with olive oil, butter, basil, parsley and tarragon. Season with pepper and sprinkle sprigs of chervil over pasta just before serving.

Fettucine with ricotta, garlic and herbs

Ricotta is a superb fresh cheese, nourishing and low in fat. Make sure it is fresh when you buy it; it is best used within two days.

SERVES 4

300–400 g (11–14 oz) fettucine
a 200 g (7 oz) wedge fresh ricotta
½ small fresh chilli, seeds removed
   (optional)
2 tbsp olive oil
2 tbsp finely cut basil leaves
1 tbsp chopped parsley
1 tsp chopped oregano
2 cloves garlic, chopped
freshly ground black pepper

METHOD

Bring a large pot of lightly salted water to the boil and cook pasta in boiling water until *al dente*.

Meanwhile, cut ricotta carefully into small cubes.

Slice chilli finely and mix with oil, basil, parsley, oregano, garlic and a little black pepper. Gently toss drained pasta with herbed oil seasoning. Serve pasta on plates and top with cubes of ricotta.

Long fusilli with zucchini and olives

I love the texture of this pasta and it is always popular with children. Choose small to medium zucchini for sweeter flavours and avoid overcooking them. The toasted pine nuts add an extra crunch.

SERVES 4

300–400 g (11–14 oz) long fusilli
10 olives, pitted
2 tbsp olive oil
2 zucchini, diced
1 tbsp Italian-style tomato sauce
2 tbsp chopped parsley
1 clove garlic, chopped
2 tbsp pine nuts, toasted
salt and freshly ground black pepper

METHOD

Bring a large pot of lightly salted water to the boil and cook pasta in boiling water until *al dente*.

Cut olives into small pieces.

Heat olive oil in a saucepan and stir-fry zucchini for 2 mins. Stir in tomato sauce, olives, parsley, garlic and pine nuts and season with salt and pepper. Toss drained pasta with zucchini mixture and serve.

Omelette with farfalle

It is easier to make a successful omelette in a non-stick pan, especially when adding other food to the egg mixture.

SERVES 2

2 tsp butter
about 100 g (3½ oz) cooked farfalle
4 eggs
salt and freshly ground black pepper
1 tbsp snipped chives

METHOD

Heat a little butter in a non-stick pan about 20 cm (about 8 in) in diameter and reheat pasta on low heat for a few mins.

Meanwhile, break eggs in a bowl and season with salt and pepper. Add chives and beat eggs with a fork for about 15 secs. Add eggs to warm pasta, increase heat and, using a wooden spoon or plastic spatula, move egg mixture around to allow it to cook rapidly. When the omelette is almost all set, turn off heat and serve.

If the pasta is a little overcooked, serve it with the sauce on top and avoid stirring it.

Spaghetti with salmon and red capsicum

Both salmon and capsicum have strong flavours that marry well with pasta. This is a lovely dish for a light lunch.

SERVES 2

1 red capiscum
200 g (7 oz) can salmon in oil
200 g (7 0z) spaghetti
1 clove garlic, chopped
2 tbsp chopped parsley
freshly ground black pepper

METHOD

Halve, seed and wash capsicum. Slice capsicum thinly.

Drain oil from salmon. Heat salmon oil in a non-stick pan. Cook capsicum on medium heat until soft.

Meanwhile, cook spaghetti in salted boiling water. Drain spaghetti and toss with capsicum, garlic, parsley and a little black pepper.

Crumble salmon over spaghetti just before serving.

Once you have added cheese to pasta, avoid mixing the dish as it becomes sticky.

Fusilli with eggplant

This dish is very popular with those who enjoy Mediterranean food. The eggplant gives it quite a rich flavour.

SERVES 2

1 tbsp olive oil
¼ onion, diced
1 small eggplant, diced
1 sprig of thyme, chopped
4 tbsp Italian-style tomato sauce
200 g (7 oz) short fusilli
1 clove garlic, chopped
1 tbsp finely sliced basil
freshly ground black pepper
freshly grated parmesan cheese

METHOD

Heat oil in a pan and stir-fry onion for 2 mins. Add eggplant and thyme and stir-fry until eggplant is soft. Stir in tomato sauce.

Meanwhile, cook pasta in lightly salted boiling water until *al dente*.

Toss drained pasta with eggplant, garlic and basil and season with freshly ground black pepper. Just before serving, add a little grated parmesan.

Use a commercially-made, plain Italian-style tomato sauce and add your own fresh herbs for a fresh touch.

Fettucine Aix-en-Provence with olives

We concocted this dish in Aix-en-Provence, the delightful town where we are living in the south of France. Here the countryside is planted with olive trees and vines from which rosé is made. Try a rosé with this tasty dish.

SERVES 2

200 g (7 oz) fettucine
1 zucchini
½ capsicum
1 tbsp olive oil
1 clove garlic, chopped
2 anchovy fillets, chopped
freshly ground black pepper
about 10 small black olives
1 tbsp chopped parsley

METHOD

Bring a large pot of lightly salted water to the boil and cook pasta in boiling water until *al dente*.

Meanwhile, cut zucchini and capsicum into small dice.

Heat olive oil in a non-stick pan and cook zucchini and capsicum for about 5 mins. Stir in garlic and anchovy fillets and season with black pepper. Toss drained pasta with vegetables, olives and chopped parsley and serve.

Remember to cook pasta in a large volume of lightly salted, boiling water.

Fettucine with fresh asparagus and button mushrooms

This is a spring pasta dish. Choose small, even asparagus spears and the smallest possible button mushrooms. I use a wok for cooking the vegetables and for tossing the cooked pasta with the vegetables. Try the fettucine verde, for a change – this is the green, spinach pasta.

SERVES ABOUT 4

300–400 g (11–14 oz) fettucine
200 g (7 oz) button mushrooms
12–16 small asparagus spears
1 tbsp vegetable oil
2 tbsp thickened cream
1 tbsp finely grated parmesan
salt and freshly ground black pepper
1 tbsp toasted pine nuts
1 tbsp finely sliced basil

METHOD

Bring a large pot of lightly salted water to the boil and cook pasta in boiling water until *al dente*.

Meanwhile, wash mushrooooms and asparagus and cut asparagus into 2 cm (about 1 in) lengths.

Heat oil in a wok and stir-fry asparagus for 1 min. Add mushrooms and cook for about 3 mins. Add cream and bring to the boil. Season with parmesan, salt and pepper. Gently toss drained pasta with vegetable sauce, pine nuts and basil and serve.

Tagliatelle with spinach and tomato

As I am very fond of spinach, this is one of my favourites and a good example of how texture is as important as flavour in cooking. You might also enjoy this dish made with bucatini, the hollow spaghetti-style pasta.

SERVES 3–4

300–400 g (11–14 oz) tagliatelle
4 cups baby spinach leaves
1 tbsp olive oil
¼ tsp curry powder
1 cup Italian-style tomato sauce
1 clove garlic, finely chopped
freshly ground black pepper
grated parmesan

METHOD

Bring a large pot of lightly salted water to the boil and cook pasta in boiling water until *al dente*.

Meanwhile, wash spinach leaves well.

Heat oil in a pan, add curry powder and spinach and cook until all the spinach is soft. Add tomato sauce and garlic and season with black pepper. Gently toss drained pasta with spinach and serve sprinkled with parmesan cheese.

When a dish of pasta tastes dull, give it some life by adding a little freshly ground black pepper, chopped parsley and chopped garlic.

Ruote di carro with peas and baby carrots

It is best to choose small peas and sweet baby carrots for this colourful dish.

SERVES 4

1 cup shelled peas
4 baby carrots
400 g (14 oz) ruote di carro (wheel-shaped
  pasta)
1 tbsp butter or olive oil
2 tbsp finely cut chives
salt and freshly ground black pepper

METHOD

Cook peas in salted boiling water.

Steam or microwave carrots then slice cooked carrots thinly.

Meanwhile, bring a large pot of lightly salted water to the boil and cook pasta in boiling water until *al dente*.

Toss drained pasta with carrots, peas, butter or olive oil and chives. Season to taste with salt and pepper.

Ruote di carro with wintry lentil sauce

Use lentils that retain their shape once cooked, such as green lentils.

SERVES 2

1 cup diced pumpkin
200 g (7 oz) ruote di carro (wheel-shaped pasta)
4 tbsp cooked lentils, canned or freshly cooked
1 tbsp olive oil
¼ tsp ground cummin
freshly ground black pepper
1 tbsp coriander leaves (optional)

METHOD

Steam or boil pumpkin until tender.

Bring a large pot of lightly salted water to the boil and cook pasta until *al dente*.

Meanwhile, drain lentils and reheat on low heat with olive oil and cummin.

Drain pasta and gently toss with lentils and cooked pumpkin. Season with pepper and serve sprinkled with coriander leaves.

The Italian cheese, pecorino, is a good substitute for parmigiano (parmesan).

Penne with borlotti beans

This hearty dish is perfect for vegetarians and has the added bonus of being both nourishing and inexpensive. You can use other beans such as cannelini or flageolets.

SERVES 4

400 g (14 oz) penne
400 g (14 oz) can borlotti beans
4 tbsp Italian-style tomato sauce
freshly ground black pepper
1 clove garlic, chopped
1 tbsp olive oil or butter
1 tbsp chopped parsley

METHOD

Cook penne in a large amount of boiling salted water until *al dente*.

Meanwhile, drain borlotti beans and discard liquid. Reheat beans with tomato sauce and season with pepper, garlic, oil or butter and parsley.

Drain cooked pasta and gently toss with beans before serving.

Have fresh basil, parsley and oregano always on hand by growing them in pots.

Penne with capsicum, bacon and anchovies

We now have a choice of many different shades of capsicum. To my taste, the red are richest in flavour. You might like to use orecchiette, the small ear-shaped pasta, for a change.

SERVES 4

1 capsicum
3 mushrooms
1 slice bacon
1 tbsp olive oil
2 anchovy fillets, cut into small pieces
400 g (14 oz) penne
1 clove garlic, chopped
2 tbsp finely sliced basil
freshly ground black pepper

METHOD

Halve, seed and dice capsicum. Cut mushrooms and bacon into small pieces.

Heat oil in a saucepan and stir-fry bacon for 1 min. Add anchovies, capsicum and mushrooms and cook until capsicum is soft.

Meanwhile, bring a large pot of lightly salted water to the boil and cook penne until *al dente*. Drain cooked pasta and place in a serving dish. Toss with capsicum preparation, chopped garlic and basil. Season with pepper and serve.

Veal ravioli with tomato and provençal herbs

In this dish I have introduced a provençal flavour by using fennel seeds and basil.

SERVES 4

about 400 g (14 oz) veal ravioli
1 tbsp olive oil
¼ tsp fennel seeds
2 cups Italian-style tomato sauce
2 tbsp finely sliced basil
1 tbsp finely sliced tarragon
freshly ground black pepper

METHOD

Bring a large saucepan of lightly salted water to the boil and cook ravioli until soft.

Meanwhile, heat olive oil in a pan, stir in fennel seeds and tomato sauce and reheat. Gently toss hot sauce with drained ravioli. Add basil and tarragon, season with black pepper and serve.

Potato gnocchi with bacon, tomato and basil

Gnocchi are now available from all pasta shops and supermarkets. Most kids love them and they cook in minutes.

SERVES 4

500 g (about 1 lb) potato gnocchi
1 tbsp olive oil
4 rashers lean bacon, finely sliced
2 cups Italian-style tomato sauce
1 tbsp finely cut basil
1 tbsp chopped parsley
1 clove garlic, chopped
freshly ground black pepper

METHOD

Bring a large saucepan of lightly salted water to the boil. Place gnocchi in boiling water and return to the boil. The gnocchi are cooked when they rise to the top and float. Once they are all floating, drain well.

Meanwhile, heat oil in a frying pan and gently fry bacon for a few mins. Add tomato sauce and bring to a simmer. Gently toss drained gnocchi with tomato sauce, basil, parsley and garlic. Season with black pepper and serve.

When using fresh herbs with pasta, avoid chopping the herbs too finely.

Capelli d'angelo in broth

This is a delicate but nourishing soup, ideal if you are feeling like a very light meal. The vegetables add goodness and flavour. If you wish, replace the capelli d'angelo (very thin, long pasta) with other thin pasta for soups.

SERVES 4

2 medium carrots
2 sticks celery
6 cups clear, strong meat or vegetable stock
salt
200 g (7 oz) capelli d'angelo
freshly ground black pepper
2 tbsp chopped parsley (optional)
1 clove garlic, chopped (optional)

METHOD

Cut carrots and celery into small pieces. Place vegetables in a saucepan with stock and a little salt, bring to the boil and cook for 10 mins. Add capelli d'angelo and cook for a few mins until just tender.

Season with pepper and stir in parsley and garlic just before serving.

Heat your pasta bowls in the oven or with hot water before serving your pasta.

PASTA FOR SPECIAL OCCASIONS

Fettucine al pesto with scallops

This is a wonderful dish for a special occasion. Choose firm fresh scallops – you may need to order them. Prepare the pesto one or several days before you need it. Alternatively, use a commercial pesto – most supermarkets and delicatessens stock good quality pesto.

SERVES 2

200 g (7 oz) fettucine
200 g (7 oz) fresh scallops
1 tbsp olive oil
8 cherry tomatoes, halved
salt and freshly ground black pepper
2 tbsp pesto sauce (see page 10)

METHOD

Bring a large pot of lightly salted water to the boil and cook pasta in boiling water until *al dente*.

Meanwhile, trim scallops of rubbery parts and remove any dark spots. Gently wash scallops, drain and dry with kitchen paper.

Heat olive oil in a non-stick frying pan and cook scallops on each side for 1 min. Add tomatoes and reheat for 30 secs. Season with a little salt and black pepper.

Drain pasta and toss gently in a serving bowl with scallops, tomatoes, and pesto then serve immediately.

Tagliatelle with smoked salmon

A dish for a feast – the smoked salmon can be replaced by smoked trout if you prefer. Avoid mixing the fish with the pasta before serving as the heat would affect the texture of the fish.

SERVES 2

about 200 g (7 oz) tagliatelle
about 90 g (about 3 oz) smoked salmon
1 tbsp sour cream
1 tbsp finely cut dill
1 tbsp finely chopped white onion
freshly ground black pepper
1 tsp butter

METHOD

Cook pasta in a large volume of lightly salted, boiling water until *al dente*.

Meanwhile, cut smoked salmon into small strips and gently mix with the sour cream, dill and white onion and season with black pepper.

Drain cooked pasta and toss with butter. Serve pasta on plates and top with smoked salmon preparation.

Noodles with curried prawns

Here is something for a special occasion. It is simple to prepare yet its exotic flavours will impress everyone. You can buy coconut cream at most supermarkets and delicatessens.

SERVES 4

1 tbsp peanut oil
½ onion, finely chopped
1 clove garlic, chopped
1 tbsp grated ginger
½ star anise
1 tbsp hot curry powder
16–20 green prawns, shelled
1 cup coconut cream
1 cup baby spinach leaves (optional)
salt
about 150 g (5½ oz) Asian noodles

METHOD

Heat oil in a wok and stir-fry onion, garlic, ginger and star anise for about 5 mins. Stir in curry powder, mix well and add prawns. Stir-fry for 1 min, add coconut cream and spinach leaves and bring to a simmer for 2 mins. Season with salt.

Meanwhile, cook the noodles in a large volume of lightly salted, boiling water. Drain cooked noodles, toss gently with prawn preparation and serve.

Rigatoni with French mustard sauce

The round, hollow rigatoni pasta is one of the most popular shapes in Italy. If you serve this with a roast, add a little gravy to the pasta sauce.

SERVES 2

200 g (7 oz) rigatoni
1 tsp butter
2 lean slices bacon, diced
2 tbsp dry white wine
2 tbsp cream
freshly ground black pepper
2 tsp Dijon mustard
1 tbsp chopped parsley (optional)

METHOD

Bring a large pot of lightly salted water to the boil and cook pasta in boiling water until *al dente*.

Meanwhile, heat butter in a non-stick frying pan and gently fry bacon for a few mins. Add white wine and bring to the boil. Add cream, return to the boil and boil for 10 secs. Season with pepper and mustard and toss the drained pasta in this sauce. Serve sprinkled with chopped parsley.

Make a thoughtful choice when shopping by carefully reading the labels of commercial pasta sauces.

Seafood bisque with conchiglie

A bisque is a seafood soup made using the shells of crustaceans. Canned varieties can be quite good and served with small pasta make a meal in a few minutes. Choose a small type of conchiglie.

SERVES 2

½ cup very small conchiglie
400 g (14 oz) can bisque (prawn or crayfish soup)
4–6 green prawns, shelled
1 tsp olive oil
1 tbsp brandy
1 clove garlic, chopped
1 tbsp chopped parsley
freshly ground black pepper

METHOD

Cook pasta in lightly salted, boiling water until *al dente*.

Meanwhile, open the can of bisque and reheat slowly. When soup is hot, lower heat to prevent it from boiling.

Add green prawns, cut into small pieces, olive oil and brandy and keep warm for 3 mins. Add small pasta, garlic and parsley and season to taste with black pepper just before serving.

Cheese ravioli with Roquefort and walnuts

Here is a dish for cheese lovers – a small serve will satisfy as it is rich. Use a blue cheese of your choice for the sauce. I love the strong flavour of Roquefort myself. Try the dish with a crunchy green salad.

SERVES 2

about 150 g (5½ oz) cheese ravioli
1 tbsp olive oil
freshly ground black pepper
50 g (about 1¾ oz) Roquefort cheese, cubed
1 tbsp walnut flesh, cut into small pieces

METHOD

Bring a pot of lightly salted water to the boil and cook ravioli until just done. Drain and place in serving dish. Toss ravioli with olive oil and season with black pepper. Sprinkle top of pasta with Roquefort and walnuts and serve.

Keep pine nuts and walnuts on hand in your pantry – they add a lovely crunch to pasta dishes.

Tortellini with mushrooms and cream

The velvety texture of mushrooms marries beautifully with pasta. Choose some of the unusual mushrooms now available for a special occasion.

SERVES 4

300 g (11 oz) tortellini
3 baby carrots
1 tsp butter
200 g (7 oz) mushrooms of your choice,
  sliced
2 tbsp cream
1 tbsp grated parmesan cheese
freshly ground black pepper

METHOD

Bring a large pot of lightly salted water to the boil and cook tortellini until just done.

Meanwhile, steam or microwave baby carrots and cut into slices.

Heat butter in a non-stick pan and sauté mushrooms until done. Stir in cream, parmesan and carrots and gently toss with drained tortellini. Season with black pepper and serve.

Grilled prosciutto with spaghetti

Prosciutto is an air-cured Italian ham. Here it is grilled until dried and crispy. Take care that it does not burn.

SERVES 2

4–6 thin slices of prosciutto
about 200 g (7 oz) spaghetti
1 tbsp olive oil
1 dried tomato, chopped
1 tbsp chopped parsley
½ tbsp finely sliced basil
1 clove garlic, chopped
freshly ground black pepper

METHOD

Place slices of prosciutto on a flat oven tray and place under a medium grill to cook and dry. Remove from heat and leave to cool. Break cooled, crisp prosciutto into pieces.

Cook pasta in lightly salted, boiling water until *al dente*.

Heat oil in a non-stick pan. Stir in dried tomato and toss in spaghetti, parsley, basil and garlic and season with pepper.

Serve sprinkled with crisp prosciutto.

Linguine with shiitake and oyster mushrooms

Mushrooms and pasta are a classic combination. The meaty texture of the various mushrooms satisfies vegetarians and meat-lovers alike. Replace the linguine with spaghetti if you wish.

SERVES 2

about 6 oyster mushrooms
3 shiitake mushrooms
1 tbsp olive oil
6 small button mushrooms
200 g (7 oz) linguine
1 clove garlic, chopped
2 tbsp chopped parsley
freshly ground black pepper

METHOD

Cut oyster mushrooms and shiitake mushrooms in half, then briefly wash them.

Heat oil in a saucepan and stir-fry the mushrooms for a few mins until soft.

Meanwhile, cook linguine in a large volume of lightly salted, boiling water until *al dente*. Drain pasta well and toss with mushrooms, garlic and parsley. Season with pepper and serve.

If you are unfamiliar with the flavour of olive oil and find it a little too strong for your taste, try a light olive oil.

ASIAN NOODLES

Asian-style duck fillet and noodles

It is now possible to buy various cuts of duck, and I make this dish with plump duck fillets. If you have time, marinate the duck for 1 hour before cooking.

SERVES 2

¼ tsp anise seeds
¼ tsp chilli paste
1 tbsp soy sauce
juice of ¼ lemon
½ tsp honey
2 plump duck fillets, skin on but without the bones
150 g (5½ oz) fresh egg noodles
salt and freshly ground black pepper
a few sprigs of coriander

METHOD

In a small bowl mix anise seeds, chilli paste, soy sauce, lemon juice and honey. Coat duck fillets with this marinade and leave to marinate for at least 10 mins.

Drain duck fillets, leaving a few anise seeds on them, if you wish, and cook under a hot grill with the skin facing upwards, for about 5 mins. Turn duck over, baste with marinade and grill for a further 2 mins. Turn again and grill, skin facing up, for a further minute.

Meanwhile, cook fresh noodles until just done in lightly salted, boiling water.

Slice cooked duck thinly and toss with noodles. Season with salt and pepper and serve sprinkled with coriander leaves.

Snow peas and sesame noodles

Those who love crisp vegetables will enjoy this lovely dish. If you wish, replace the snow peas with Chinese broccoli or cabbage.

SERVES 2

150 g (5½ oz) snow peas
1 tbsp peanut oil
½ small clove garlic, finely chopped
2 tbsp water
100 g (3½ oz) egg noodles
½ tsp sesame oil
½ tbsp soy sauce
¼ tsp chilli paste (optional)
1 tsp sesame seeds

METHOD

Top and tail snow peas and wash in icy cold water.

Heat peanut oil in a wok. When hot, add garlic and snow peas and stir-fry for 1 min. Add water to wok, cover and steam for 30 secs.

Meanwhile, cook egg noodles in a large volume of salted, boiling water. Drain noodles.

Season snow peas with sesame oil, soy sauce and chilli paste and gently toss with noodles. Sprinkle with sesame seeds just before serving.

Chilli chicken wings with noodles

I am very fond of chicken wings. Trim them of as much fat as possible before cooking.

SERVES 2

1 small, hot red chilli pepper
1 tbsp peanut oil
10 chicken wings, trimmed
about 6 fennel seeds or anise seeds
1 clove garlic, chopped
1 tbsp soy sauce
2 tbsp dry sherry
1 tbsp honey
½ tsp sesame oil
about 100 g (3½ oz) dried Chinese noodles

METHOD

Halve chilli pepper, remove seeds and slice finely.

Heat peanut oil in a wok and stir-fry chicken wings for about 5 mins. Add chilli, fennel seeds and garlic and stir for 10 secs. Add soy sauce, sherry, honey and sesame oil. Stir well, reduce heat, cover and cook for a further 10 mins, stirring occasionally.

Meanwhile, cook noodles in lightly salted, boiling water.

Toss drained noodles with chicken wings and serve.

Chinese pork with fresh egg noodles

In Chinese grocery shops and restaurant windows you have probably noticed the very appetising roast meat. Roast pork is always there. Buy a piece and try this recipe for a really quick Asian noodle dish.

SERVES 3

a 200 g (7 oz) piece of roast pork
½ tbsp peanut oil
about 20 anise seeds
1 cup bean shoots
200 g (7 oz) fresh egg noodles
1 tbsp soy sauce
a few drops sesame oil
a few sprigs of coriander

METHOD

Cut pork into thin slices.

Heat oil in a wok, stir in anise seeds and stir-fry pork for 30 secs. Add bean shoots and stir-fry for a few mins until just soft.

Meanwhile, cook egg noodles in lightly salted, boiling water.

Toss drained noodles with pork preparation, soy sauce and sesame oil and serve topped with coriander.

A non-stick saucepan is a perfect utensil for tossing pasta with a sauce.

Vietnamese prawn and noodle soup

The Vietnamese make a meal of a noodle soup. Adapt this recipe to your taste by using other seafood or meat instead of prawns. The cellophane noodles are soaked in water before being added to the other ingredients.

SERVES ABOUT 4

8–16 green prawns, shelled and deveined
½ tsp finely grated ginger
1 tbsp Asian fish sauce (nam pla)
¼ tsp turmeric
¼ small fresh chilli, finely sliced (optional)
about 40 g (1⅓ oz) cellophane noodles
½ tbsp vegetable oil
½ onion, chopped
1 clove garlic, chopped
½ tsp dried shrimp paste
4 cups hot water
freshly ground black pepper
1 tsp lemon juice
8 small mint leaves, left whole
½ cup bean shoots

METHOD

Cut prawns into small pieces and place in a bowl with ginger, fish sauce, turmeric and chilli.

Soak noodles in a bowl of hot water for 10 mins.

Heat oil in a saucepan and gently fry onion and garlic for about 5 mins. Stir in shrimp paste and cook for 30 secs before adding hot water and drained noodles. Bring to the boil and boil for about 3 mins. Add prawns and sauce, simmer for 30 secs, season with pepper and lemon juice and serve with mint leaves and bean shoots.

Thai green chicken curry with rice noodles

This is a Thai-style dish with short cuts for the busy cook. You will find green curry paste in your supermarket, and on the way home, get a roast chicken from your local chicken shop. The coriander leaves add a lovely fresh, peppery taste.

SERVES 4–6

3 cups coconut cream
2 tbsp green curry paste
about 60 g (2 oz) rice noodles
1 roast chicken
1 tbsp Asian fish sauce (nam pla)
½ cup coriander leaves

METHOD

Bring coconut cream and curry paste to a simmer in a non-stick pan, stirring occasionally.

Soak rice noodles in a bowl of hot water for about 10 mins.

Meanwhile, using a cleaver, cut chicken into small pieces, keeping it on the bone. Add chicken to coconut cream mixture and reheat on low heat. Stir fish sauce into chicken.

Place drained noodles in a deep serving dish and top with chicken and sauce. Sprinkle coriander leaves over chicken and serve.

Stir-fried beef and capsicum with noodles

Here is a tasty and satisfying dish which you can easily vary simply by changing the spices. You'll find fresh Asian noodles in the refrigerated section of Asian grocery stores.

SERVES 2

1 tbsp peanut oil
1 red capsicum, cut into strips
100 g (3½ oz) fresh Asian noodles
1 clove garlic, chopped
½ small fresh chilli, cut into small pieces
250 g (9 oz) beef fillet, cut into strips
2 tbsp soy sauce
½ tsp sesame oil

METHOD

Heat half of the peanut oil in a wok and on high heat stir-fry capsicum until soft. Transfer capsicum to a plate.

Cook pasta in a large volume of lightly salted, boiling water. Drain well.

Heat remaining oil in wok. Stir in garlic and chilli, add beef strips and, on high heat, stir-fry until meat has changed colour. Take care not to overcook meat.

Gently toss noodles with capsicum, beef, soy sauce and sesame oil and serve.

Sweet and sour pork with noodles

For best results use a wok for this dish. I like to use thin, dried Asian noodles which are available in all supermarkets. If you have time, marinate the pork for 2 hours in advance.

SERVES 2

150 g (5½ oz) pork fillet
½ tbsp honey
juice of ½ lemon
¼ tsp chilli paste
1 tsp grated ginger
1 clove garlic, finely chopped
1 tbsp soy sauce
1 tsp corn flour
about 100 g (3½ oz) Asian noodles
2 tbsp peanut oil

METHOD

Cut pork into thin slices.

In a bowl combine honey, lemon, chilli paste, ginger, garlic, soy sauce and corn flour. Stir in pork and leave to marinate.

Cook Asian noodles in lightly salted, boiling water until soft. Drain.

Heat oil in a wok and stir-fry pork quickly on high heat until just done. Toss drained noodles with pork and serve.

Reheat cold cooked pasta in a large amount of hot water, not boiling water or it will cook further, for a few minutes. Then drain and mix with sauce or seasoning.

Stir-fried chicken with green beans and noodles

I use the fresh noodles that can be found in the refrigerated section of Asian grocery shops and some supermarkets. For best results use a wok or large non-stick frying pan.

SERVES 2

200 g (7 oz) chicken meat, cut into strips
1 tsp corn flour
2 tbsp soy sauce
150 g (5½ oz) French beans
about 150 g (5½ oz) fresh Asian noodles
1½ tbsp peanut oil
1 thin slice of ginger
1 clove garlic, chopped
¼ tsp sesame oil
½ tsp chilli paste
a few drops lemon juice
freshly ground black pepper

METHOD

In a small bowl mix chicken strips with corn flour and half of the soy sauce.

Steam or microwave beans until just crunchy.

Cook noodles in a large pot of lightly salted, boiling water.

Heat peanut oil in wok. Stir in slice of ginger and garlic and stir-fry chicken until it changes colour. Add beans and mix well. Season with remaining soy sauce, sesame oil, chilli paste, lemon juice and a little black pepper. Gently toss drained noddles with chicken and serve.

Singapore noodles

Every family in Singapore would have its own version of this flavoursome and satisfying dish. You'll need to visit a Chinese grocer to obtain the ingredients, especially the roast pork and the Chinese sausage.

SERVES 2

100 g (3½ oz) fresh Asian noodles
1 tbsp oil
1 thin slice of ginger
1 clove garlic, chopped
1 tsp curry powder
1 cup finely sliced celery
1 cup diced carrot
½ cup cooked shrimps
½ cup Chinese roast pork, finely sliced
1 small Chinese sausage
½ cup bean sprouts
1 hard-boiled egg, cut into pieces
1 tbsp soy sauce
2 spring onions, cut into small pieces
a few sprigs of coriander

METHOD

Place fresh Asian noodles in boiling water for 1 min then drain.

Heat oil in a wok and stir-fry ginger, garlic, curry powder, celery and carrot for 1 min. Add shrimps, pork and sausage and stir-fry for 1 min. Add bean sprouts and stir-fry for about 30 secs. Gently toss in noodles and egg, season with soy sauce and spring onion and serve sprinkled with coriander sprigs.

If not serving immediately, keep your dish of pasta warm, covered with foil in the oven at 100°C/200°F.

My Thai noodles

Thais and other Asians use flat rice noodles with a slippery texture that are really lovely with the freshest of green vegetables, such as Chinese cabbage.

SERVES 4

about 100 g (3½ oz) flat rice noodles
2 tbsp peanut oil
2 eggs, lightly beaten
4 fresh shiitake mushrooms, sliced
1 cup shredded Chinese cabbage
½ small, hot red chilli
1 tbsp grated ginger
1 clove garlic, chopped
1 chicken fillet, finely sliced
½ cup cooked shrimps
1 tbsp soy sauce
1 tbsp oyster sauce
2 tsp fish sauce (nam pla)
1 tsp sugar
4 spring onions, cut into small pieces

METHOD

Cook rice noodles briefly in boiling water and drain.

Heat ½ tbsp oil in wok and make a quick omelette with the eggs. Transfer omelette to a plate, then slice it into strips.

Heat another ½ tbsp oil in wok and stir-fry mushrooms and cabbage until soft. Transfer to a plate. Heat remaining oil in wok and stir in chilli, ginger and garlic. Add chicken and stir-fry for 1 min before adding shrimps, soy sauce, oyster sauce, fish sauce and sugar. Add vegetables, omelette strips and cooked rice noodles to pan and reheat, tossing well. Serve sprinkled with pieces of spring onion on top.

Indonesian noodles with fresh vegetables

This is a version of Bami, one of my favourite Indonesian noodle dishes. Use dried or fresh noodles.

SERVES 4

about 150 g (3½ oz) Asian noodles
2 tbsp peanut oil
1 lean rasher bacon, chopped
¼ onion, chopped
1 clove garlic, chopped
1 tsp grated ginger
½ cup chopped carrot
½ cup chopped celery
1 cup shredded cabbage
2 tbsp water
2 tbsp soy sauce
1 tsp chilli paste
1 hard-boiled egg, chopped

METHOD

Cook noodles in a large pot of lightly salted, boiling water. Drain well.

Heat half the oil in a wok and stir-fry bacon for 2 mins. Transfer bacon to a plate. Add remaining oil to wok and stir in onion, garlic and ginger. Add carrot and celery and stir-fry for a few mins until vegetables start to soften. Add cabbage and stir-fry for 1 min before adding the water. Cover with a lid and steam for a few mins until cabbage starts to soften but still has a little crunch. Stir soy sauce and chilli paste into vegetables and toss gently with noodles, egg and bacon before serving.

COUSCOUS

Couscous with Moroccan chicken and vegetables

I prefer using chicken thighs or drumsticks to chicken fillets in this rustic dish which is full of colour and flavour. Harissa is a hot chilli paste. Some supermarkets carry it, or try a Middle Eastern grocery shop.

SERVES 4

4–8 pieces of skinned chicken on the bone
2 turnips, halved and peeled
4 whole baby carrots, peeled
4 leaves of silverbeet, cut in pieces
1 tsp ground cummin
1 tbsp tomato paste
1 tsp harissa (hot chilli paste)
1 tbsp olive oil
1 clove garlic, crushed
1 cup Italian-style tomato sauce
3 cups water

| salt and freshly ground black pepper
| a 1.5 cm (about ¾ in) piece of cinnamon
| 400 g (14 oz) couscous

METHOD

Place chicken pieces, turnips, carrots, silverbeet, cummin, tomato paste, harissa, olive oil, garlic, tomato sauce and water in a large saucepan. Season with salt and pepper, bring to the boil and simmer for 15 mins. Add cinnamon and simmer for an extra 5 mins. Remove cinnamon stick.

Meanwhile, cook couscous according to packet instructions.

Serve chicken and vegetables in one dish and the couscous in another and place in the centre of the table for all to help themselves.

Vegetarian couscous

Here is a very satisfying treat. Choose seasonal vegetables – root vegetables are particularly good.

SERVES 4

2 carrots, cut in half across
2 turnips, peeled and halved
1 red capsicum, seeded and cut in four
2 zucchini, cut in half across
1 tbsp tomato paste
3 tomatoes, quartered
1 tsp harissa (hot chilli paste)
1 tsp ground cummin
1 clove garlic, crushed
1 tbsp olive oil
3 cups water
salt and freshly ground black pepper
400 g (14 oz) can chick peas, drained
300 g (11 oz) couscous
a few sprigs of coriander

METHOD

In a saucepan place carrots, turnips, capsicum, zucchini, tomato paste, tomato quarters, harissa, cummin, garlic, olive oil and water and season with a little salt and pepper. Bring to the boil and cook for 10 mins on high heat. Add drained chick peas and cook for a further 10 mins. Meanwhile, cook couscous according to packet instructions.

Serve couscous and vegetables, topped with sprigs of coriander, from the centre of the table for all to help themselves.

Couscous with seafood

It is best to use a firm fish for this superb dish. Ask your fishmonger to scale and clean the fish, to remove the head and cut the fish into 5 cm (about 2 in) cutlets. This is a wonderful dish to share with friends – serve it in large bowls in the centre of the table for all to help themselves.

SERVES ABOUT 4

1 kg (about 2 lb) firm fish, cut in 5 cm (about 2 in) cutlets (gurnard, flathead, leatherjacket)
1 red capsicum, cut into 8 pieces
3 silverbeet leaves, cut into pieces
2 zucchini, cut into 8 pieces
1 tbsp tomato paste
1 cup Italian-style tomato sauce
1 tsp harissa (hot chilli paste)
¼ tsp fennel seeds
1 tsp ground cummin
1 clove garlic, crushed
1 tbsp olive oil

4 cups water
about 8 shelled green prawns
salt and freshly ground black pepper
about 300 g (11 oz) couscous

METHOD

Place fish, capsicum, silverbeet, zucchini, tomato paste, tomato sauce, harissa, fennel seeds, cummin, garlic, olive oil and water in a saucepan. Bring to the boil and simmer for 10 mins. Add prawns, simmer for 30 secs and turn off heat. Season with salt and pepper.

Meanwhile, cook couscous according to packet instructions.

Serve couscous and seafood stew from the centre of the table in two deep dishes.

Couscous salad for a barbecue

This one is easy to prepare for a large number of people, and it keeps well. For a barbecue, an original salad is always popular.

SERVES 8

about 500 g (about 1 lb) couscous
juice of 1 lemon
salt and freshly ground black pepper
about 8 mint leaves, finely sliced
3 spring onions, finely sliced
3 tbsp olive oil
4 tomatoes, diced
1 cup cucumber, diced
1 cup drained, cooked chick peas (from a
can)

METHOD

Cook couscous according to packet instructions and allow to cool in a large dish.

In a large salad bowl, mix lemon juice with a little salt and freshly ground black pepper, the mint leaves, spring onion and olive oil. Add diced tomato, cucumber and chick peas then toss gently with the cold couscous.

Keep covered and refrigerated if not using immediately.

INDEX

Asian-style duck fillet and noodles, 96

Capelli d'angelo in broth, 76

Cheese ravioli with Roquefort and walnuts, 88

Chilli chicken wings with noodles, 100

Chinese pork with fresh egg noodles, 102

Couscous salad for a barbecue, 126

Couscous with Moroccan chicken and vegetables, 120

Couscous with seafood, 124

Fast spaghetti bolognese, 30

Fettucine Aix-en-Provence with olives, 58

Fettucine al pesto with scallops, 78

Fettucine with fresh asparagus and button mushrooms, 60

Fettucine with ricotta, garlic and herbs, 48

Fusilli with eggplant, 56

Garlic and parsley sauce, 15

Gnocchi with tomato and pine nuts, 38

Grilled prosciutto with spaghetti, 92

Indonesian noodles with fresh vegetables, 118

Italian tomato sauce, 16

Linguine with shiitake and oyster mushrooms, 94

Long fusilli with tuna and capers, 34

Long fusilli with zucchini and olives, 50

Macaroni au gratin, 24

Macaroni with stir-fried beef, 28

Matriciana sauce, 14

Mexican bean sauce, 12

My Thai noodles, 116

Noodles with curried prawns, 82

Omelette with farfalle, 52

Penne with borlotti beans, 68

Penne with capsicum, bacon and anchovies, 70

Penne with sun-dried tomatoes and basil, 26

Pesto Genovese, 10

Potato gnocchi with bacon, tomato and basil, 74

Ricotta ravioli with ham, 36

Rigatoni with French mustard sauce, 84

Rigatoni with soy chicken, 40

Ruote di carro with peas and baby carrots, 64

Ruote di carro with wintry lentil sauce, 66

Seafood bisque with conchiglie, 86

Singapore noodles, 114

Snow peas and sesame noodles, 98

Spaghetti alla carbonara, 18

Spaghetti alla puttanesca, 22

Spaghetti with fresh seafood, 20

Spaghetti with salmon and red capsicum, 54

Spaghettini with fine herbs and garlic, 46

Spaghettini with ginger and chilli, 32

Stir-fried beef and capsicum with noodles, 108

Stir-fried chicken with green beans and noodles, 112

Sweet and sour pork with noodles, 110

Tagliatelle with chicken livers, 42

Tagliatelle with smoked salmon, 80

Tagliatelle with spicy minced beef, 44

Tagliatelle with spinach and tomato, 62

Thai green chicken curry with rice noodles, 106

Tortellini with mushrooms and cream, 90

Veal ravioli with tomato and provençal herbs, 72

Vegetarian couscous, 122

Vietnamese prawn and noodle soup, 104